It's OK to Share a Secret

Amber Donaldson

Copyright © *Amber Donaldson*, 2024

All Rights Reserved

This book is subject to the condition that no part of this book is to be reproduced, transmitted in any form or means; electronic or mechanical, stored in a retrieval system, photocopied, recorded, scanned, or otherwise. Any of these actions require the proper written permission of the author.

To those who I told my secrets to, thank you – you know who you are.

Sammie is so excited to be working on her secret present, in Mrs. Johnston's class today. The class is painting clay pots with their mommy's favorite colors and will be planting flower seeds to grow, just in time for Mother's Day. During dinner that evening, Sammie shared what the class was working on that day and realized she spilled the beans to her mommy. OOPS!

The next day in class, they continued to work on their presents and Mrs. Johnston could see that Sammie wasn't as excited as the day before. Mrs. Johnston asked Sammie what was wrong and if she would like to talk. Sammie looked up with tears in her eyes and said, "I ruined the surprise for my Mommy, I told her about the secret present". Mrs. Johston told Sammie that it was okay that she told her mommy about the present. Some secrets are hard to keep but it's okay to share them, and that her mommy will still be surprised once she sees it on Mother's Day.

To add to the Mother's Day present, Sammie and her little brother were making some bead jewelry. He finished his part and hurried to go play in his room. A few nights later, his nose was hurting him badly and he couldn't breathe very well so mommy and daddy had to bring him to the doctors. The doctor found one of the beads stuck in his nose. After a few tries, the doctor was able to get it out, and said "beads do not belong in our noses".

On their way home, mommy asked him why he put a bead up his nose and didn't tell someone that it was stuck? My little brother said he was scared that he would get into trouble and kept it a secret. Daddy chimed in saying that whenever you are hurting, you should never keep it a secret, always tell an adult. My brother agreed to never put anything up his nose again, not even his finger!

Today Sammie and her little brother were spending the day with their grandparents, while their mommy and daddy were at work. It was a whole day of fun, playing outside, reading books, watering the plants, and listening to grandpa complain about a project he was working on that is going wrong. Well, it was time to go home, and grandpa asked if they would like to have dessert before dinner. Of course, Sammie and her little brother said YES! Grandpa brought them to get ice cream before going home, but said "this is our little secret, I don't want mommy to be mad at me for ruining your appetite for dinner".

That evening it was Sammie's favorite dinner, spaghetti, but she wasn't eating very much. Her daddy asked why she wasn't hungry, and she said it's because she was still full, from the big ice cream cone. OOPS...Sammie spilled the beans about grandpa's secret! Sammie's mommy and daddy looked at each other and laughed, saying "of course grandpa brought you for ice cream before dinner, that's what grandpa's do". Sammie was relieved that she didn't get grandpa in trouble for telling their secret. Phew!

Back at school, Sammie's best friend in Mrs. Johnston's class is Denise, they love all the same stuff, and do the same things. Sammie saw that Denise has been very sad lately and one day Denise was all by herself, crying on the playground. Sammie went over to be with Denise and asked her what was wrong. Denise wipe tears from her eyes and asked, "can you keep a secret?", of course Sammie told her best friend yes. Denise told her that her uncle has been living with them for a little while and has been tickling her a lot. He told Denise that it was their secret tickle time and not to tell anyone, but Denise's belly didn't feel right, and it wasn't fun at all. Sammie told Denise that if she doesn't like to be tickled, then ask him to stop, and if he doesn't then tell your mommy.

The next morning when Sammie was getting ready for school, she asked her mommy "when is it okay to share a secret?" Mommy told her that she could share a secret whenever she would like, especially if a secret is making her worry and feeling sick to her belly. Sometimes secrets are accidentally shared when you are so excited about it, like giving someone a present, but it's still okay to share it.

A few days went by, and Denise was still really sad. Sammie was now sad for her best friend too. Sammie couldn't keep the secret any longer and told their teacher. Mrs. Johston told Sammie that she did a very brave thing by telling her about Denise, and that she should always share a secret if someone is sad or getting hurt. It's always best by saying something and not keeping it to ourselves.

Denise was not at school for a little while and she finally came back! Sammie hugged Denise as soon as she walked through the classroom door, and she was happy again. She said that she had to talk to a lady about the secret tickle time and now her uncle no longer lives at their house! Sammie was so happy for her friend Denise, that she couldn't wait to get home and tell her mommy and daddy.

That evening at dinner, Sammie told her mommy and daddy all about Denise and how happy she was again. They were so proud of Sammie for standing up and sharing Denise's secret, they said on Saturday they were taking Denise and Sammie to the trampoline park for the day and then for a sleepover! This was the best news ever and Sammie could not wait to spend the whole day with her best friend!

Secrets can make you feel happy, excited, sad, scared, and even hurt, but always know never be afraid to share one whether you meant to or not. If you are asked to keep a secret from someone who is supposed to love you and it makes your belly feel yucky, then make sure to tell an adult who you trust.

My friends, there is always someone close to share

a secret with, no matter how it makes you feel. Just

know you are a brave one!

Thank you for being you ♡

Now it's Your Turn to Share!

Have you ever shared a secret with a friend or kept one for them?

Think about the times you've trusted someone with something special or helped a friend.

Use this space to write down your thoughts and memories! ⭐

_____

_____

_____

_____

_____

_____

_____

www.ingramcontent.com/pod-product-compliance
Lightning Source LLC
Chambersburg PA
CBHW081629100526
44590CB00021B/3663